P9-CQG-662

RESPICE STELLAM

THE SACRIFICE OF THE CHURCH

THE SACRIFICE OF THE CHURCH

The Meaning of the Mass

by

Joseph A. Jungmann, S.J.

Translated from the German by
CLIFFORD HOWELL, S.J.

LITURGICAL PRESS
COLLEGEVILLE, MINNESOTA

Originally published in German
by Johannes-Verlag, Basel
under the title 'Vom Sinn der Messe als
Opfer der Gemeinschaft'

Conceditur P. CLIFFORD HOWELL, S.J., facultas edendi librum cui titulas *The Sacrifice of the Church*

D. BOYLE, S.J.
Praep. Prov. Angl. Soc. Jesu
Die: 20 Decembris 1955

Nihil Obstat: DERMITIUS FOGARTY, S.T.D.
Censor Deputatus

Imprimatur: *Datum Southwarci: die 26a Junii 1956*
H. GIBNEY
Vic. Gen.

PRINTED IN GREAT BRITAIN BY
THE DITCHLING PRESS LTD
DITCHLING, SUSSEX

CONTENTS

I

THE SACRIFICE OF THE CHURCH

FROM the times of the Apostles until today the Holy Eucharist has ever been acknowledged as the most precious of all the treasures entrusted for preservation to the Church. The altar is the focal point of the House of God, and the Sunday Mass is the greatest event of the week; so it has ever been.

But it is altogether another question whether at all times, including the present, this treasure has been fully used and rendered as fruitful as possible for the spiritual life of succeeding generations. If we study the rich content of the Eucharistic mystery and the stimulating power inherent in the liturgy of the Mass we cannot but admit that success in this matter has been only partial. In particular it is worth while devoting some attention to the thought that the Mass is not only the sacrifice of Christ but also the sacrifice of the Church.

The liturgy of the Mass appears to have suffered a fate very like that of many an ancient building which, in the course of centuries, has been enlarged and adapted to make it suitable for new purposes. In such a case it may well happen that, with changed conditions and style of living, people hardly know what to do with certain parts of the building. They may end up by dwelling in only a small part of the whole complex structure, while the remaining parts become uninhabited.

This is what has happened to the liturgy of the Mass. The fact stands out when we compare all its riches with those aspects of it which alone remain as live elements in popular piety and are given prominence in devotional writings: there are whole regions of it which remain uninhabited.

Indeed what the catechism teaches us about the Mass is all perfectly true; here are the very thoughts and concepts which we find in the treatises of dogmatic theology. But this is not an unmixed advantage: it implies also a weakness. The advantage is that we have a warrant for the basic thoughts and concepts in terms of which the essence of the sacred mystery is, to some extent, expressible: the real presence of our Lord under the two species, the reality of the sacrifice, the re-enactment of Calvary. The weakness is that these thoughts and concepts are only the basis; we cling to ideas crystallised out by the controversies which arose in the sixteenth century.[1] Of all the heritage of previous ages (that which chiefly finds expression in the liturgy) there remains very much of great importance which is ignored.

Periods of strife and controversy always have an unfortunate consequence; the defendant must at all costs save the point attacked, and so this threatened point is stressed while others are passed over. This was so when the Reformers of the sixteenth century attacked the

1 See the very important chapter by Fr X. Arnold, *Vorgeschichte und Einfluss des Trienter Messopferdekrets auf die Behandlung des eucharistischen Geheimnisses in der Glaubensverkündigung der Neuzeit.* To be found in the book *Die Messe in der Glaubensverkündigung* edited by Fr X. Arnold and Balthazar Fischer, Freiburg 1950, pp. 114-161.

Catholic doctrine of the sacrificial nature of the Mass. They maintained that the Mass was not a sacrifice, not an action whereby we might please God. Catholic theologians therefore rallied to the defence of sacrifice; they concentrated on that point which lies at the very centre of Catholic sacrificial teaching and which can most easily be defended because there is biblical warrant for it. They showed that the Mass is the sacrifice of Christ, the renewal of his sacrifice on the Cross; that on the altar we have, through the institution of Christ, his own Flesh and Blood under the distinct species which of themselves manifest that the Mass is a sacrifice. Hence the Council of Trent teaches that in the Mass the same High Priest is active as on Calvary, namely, Christ himself who now offers himself here as he did there, only the manner of offering being different.

By this means the central point of Catholic teaching and practice concerning the Mass was certainly endorsed and assured for the faithful. And when Catholic piety centres itself with especial love upon this thought and draws devotion from it, this is beyond question a sound and solid piety. The faithful grasp that in the Mass the sacrifice of the Cross is renewed; that it is the memorial of the Passion of Christ. Already in the Middle Ages popular devotion to the Mass had been occupied before all else precisely with this thought. The people had, in fact, learned to regard the entire celebration of the Mass as a drama portraying the life and sufferings of Jesus. Every little detail was seen as a representation of some event in the life of our Lord from his birth right up till his resurrection and ascension into heaven. These are the thoughts which were ever revived and perpetuated.

But what was grasped even more vividly was the doctrine that on the altar a genuine sacrifice takes place, a sacrifice offered by Christ himself for the 'four ends' of adoration, thanksgiving, petition and propitiation. And thus it was a favourite practice to offer the Mass to the Heavenly Father to adore him and thank him, to pray for all things needful and to make reparation for the sins of the world.

There was also a third aspect which claimed an ever-increasing attention, a thought which also was strongly emphasised towards the end of the Middle Ages, namely, that in the Mass Christ himself is really present; in the Mass one can adore him and pray to him. And so there became established ever more and more the practice of exposing the Blessed Sacrament upon the altar throughout the whole of the Mass.

As we have said, it is indeed a well-based form of piety if people take part in the Mass in this fashion. But one must also add the remark that it does not by any means make full use of the content of the Mass. For in this way the real meaning of the celebration of the Mass and of its liturgy cannot be clearly grasped. What, after all, was the purpose which our Lord had in mind when he gave us the Mass? Certainly not just that we who are born in later days might have the opportunity of being present at his sacrifice and thus of sharing in its fruits. What he intended was rather this: that we might be able to offer together with him this sacrifice which he was making available to us in all places and at all times. On the Cross he offered all alone; but on the altar he desired that his Church should offer in union with him. On the altar he would bring to pass his own words: 'I, if I be lifted up from the earth, will attract all men to myself' (John 12, 32). On the altar he would draw his faithful into his own dispositions, into his obedience, into his self-giving to the Father, into his spirit of sacrifice. In short: on the altar his Church should offer sacrifice with him.

This corresponds absolutely with the understanding of this matter which the Church had in her earliest period. Even in times before the Reformation, when the stream of thought about the Mass was running undisturbed in the channel of tradition, it was a customary mode of expression to say 'The Church offers; we offer'. In fact leading theologians were even of the opinion that a priest who had been excommunicated, and thus cut off from the Church, was thereby rendered incapable of consecrating validly because he could no longer say the word *offerimus* in the name of the Church.[2] The Council of Trent reminds us that Christ 'according to the needs of human nature, has left to his beloved spouse, the Church, a visible sacrifice'. It is to the Church that Christ has handed over his holy sacrifice; she is to have it and to offer it together with Christ her Bridegroom. But very little was said about all this, because it was taken for granted. In theological treatises there is but small mention of the fact that it is the Church which offers the Mass with Christ.

2 This was the opinion, for example, of Peter Lombard.

The language of the liturgy is much more explicit. And so if we approach the liturgy of the Mass from the viewpoint of the train of thought embodied in our theological treatises on the Mass and expressed also in our catechisms, we experience a kind of tension—almost a discrepancy. The fact is that what we view from the standpoint of our dogmatic treatise and what has taken shape in the liturgy are really the same thing. But as we approach it from different angles it presents to us two different appearances.

This is specially striking when we come to examine the basic plan of our Mass-liturgy as it was devised in the earliest days of the Church. One of the oldest names used to describe the celebration is *Eucharistia*, Thanksgiving. This name was given precisely because the liturgy of the Mass, since its origin in the first century, took the form of thanksgiving. In those days there was no Fore-mass; the preparation of the gifts took place without any particular formalities. The celebration began with the summons: *Gratias agamus Domino Deo nostro*, 'Let us give thanks to the Lord our God'. Then followed immediately the prayer of thanksgiving, as described to us by Justin Martyr—that which was called the *eucharistia*. We have the actual text of such a eucharistic prayer from a date which is only a little later, about the year 200 A.D.[3] It is an expression of thanks for the mercies of God who sent us his Son that he might free us from the power of sin and of Satan. Then follows the account of the Last Supper; the words of consecration are spoken; and the expression

3 The *Eucharistia* of Hippolytus of Rome.

of thanks is transformed into the act of offering. *Gratias agamus* becomes *offerimus*. The Church offers sacrifice, and Communion follows.

If we study this groundplan of the Mass, evolved in the early Church and still underlying the Mass-liturgy of today, we perceive that we are yet one step further removed from the train of thought to which our theological view of the Mass had made us accustomed. For the celebration, taken as a whole, does not even appear primarily under the aspect of sacrifice; it appears directly as a thanksgiving—a thanksgiving, moreover, which is rendered to God by the Church. First, then, we must face the question: Why primarily as thanksgiving, and not immediately as sacrifice? Only when we have answered that can we proceed to the second question: Why the sacrifice of the Church? Why and in what sense does the liturgy stress the sacrifice of the Church and not the sacrifice of Christ?

Why, then, thanksgiving and not immediately sacrifice? This seeming contradiction is not difficult to reconcile. In the first place the disposition of gratitude is to be awakened and expressed. This happens in the eucharistic prayer. But it does not follow that gratitude is expressible only in words; for the very words of thanks can themselves find a further expression in the action of gift-giving. Much the same happens when we desire to honour some public benefactor: we propose to him a vote of thanks and make to him a presentation. But the speech of thanks will not be all about the gift which is to be presented to him; it will concern itself rather with all those good deeds of his for which he is now being thanked. So it is also in the celebration of the Eucharist; the real Eucharist begins with a formal speech of thanks, a thanksgiving prayer. And from this prayer of thanksgiving there originates the offering: *Te igitur rogamus ac petimus uti accepta habeas*, 'We pray and beseech thee graciously to accept'.

Besides this we must hold in mind that the prevailing circumstances of those times impelled the early Christians to lay stress on interior dispositions rather than on outward acts, on interior gratitude rather than on exterior sacrifice. Both the heathens and the Jews believed that they were pleasing God by their external achievements; they sought in various ways to increase the quantity and material value of their sacrificial offerings. Christians, by contrast, had but one sacrificial gift, of a spiritual nature, in which the material element was of slight importance. The value of it lay in holy dispositions, in interior self-giving to God, in gratitude for favours received.

Moreover the Christian sacrifice has been instituted as a memorial—a memorial of Christ, of his redeeming passion and glorious resurrection by means of which he has opened to us the way of eternal life. So the Christian sacrifice is embedded in a prayer of thanksgiving: it begins with the thanks of the assembled community, the Church, and out of this the offering of the Church develops. Thus the liturgy of Holy Mass is shaped in a basic form such that the sacrifice of the Church does, in fact, find expression in it. The sacrifice of Christ is also here—it appears as the central element of the celebration in the consecration. At this point the priest, who till then has formulated the prayer of the assembled community as its spokesman, suddenly begins to act in the role of Christ who renews his own sacrifice through him. The priest does not only speak words of consecration; also he performs accompanying actions which express in the clearest possible manner that he is now intending to do what Christ has done and desires to do anew through his ministry: he takes the bread, he takes also the chalice, he looks up to heaven. The oriental liturgies go even further and arrange that at this point the priest shall also imitate Christ in the breaking of the bread. It is manifest that Christ is renewing his sacrifice through the ministry of his priest.

And yet this central element of the celebration is enclosed within a very varied envelope. It is completely surrounded by prayers and ceremonies which all serve to express the praying and sacrificing of the Church. They constitute an ascent of many steps which the Church mounts until the heights of the consecration are attained. There is the humble cleansing from sin in the priest's public confession of guilt, the hearing of God's word in the Scripture readings, the preparation of the gifts which, even in their natural condition, show forth homage to the Creator; then there is the great prayer of thanksgiving and the triple *Sanctus* in which the praises of heaven are united with those of earth. Thus does the Church climb up towards her Lord, *in montem sanctum tuum et in tabernacula tua* (Ps. 42, 3). And here she meets her Lord who now offers his own sacrifice with her. For the priest who at that moment stands at the altar as the representative of Christ does not thereby cease to be also the representative of the Church. It is the Church which sent him forth and, in a sense, commissioned him to step forward on her behalf in the service of Christ. It is rather like what happens when a child puts his little hands in between the folded hands of his mother while both of them say a prayer together.

But as regards external form, in those elements which are visible, we find that after the consecration it is once more the Church's sacrifice—and this alone—which is brought into the foreground. '*We* offer'—*offerimus praeclarae majestati tuae*. We range our sacrifice in the series of great sacrifices of the Old Testament—the sacrifices of Abel, of Abraham and of Melchisedech. Certainly we know that the value of our gift far surpasses any of theirs; but at the same time we are conscious that we are but poor children of Eve who with our own unworthy hands are offering this great gift to God; realising also that our unworthiness is capable of obscuring the glory of this our gift.

And now comes another point we should think about: What exactly is this 'Church' who is offering? Does the word mean always the Universal Church which, through her priestly ministers, offers the One Sacrifice in a thousand places throughout the world? or does it mean just the priest who is here and now her representative?—and that the faithful are merely called on to be present as witnesses who follow the course of the Mass with devotion? We can be certain that this is far too narrow a view. No doubt the Church Militant does stand behind the sacrifice of the priest. He must be authorised by and have faculties from the bishop, and the bishop himself must pertain to the hierarchic organism of the worldwide Church. That is why at every Mass the offering is made *in primis pro Ecclesia tua sancta catholica*, 'in the first place for thy holy Catholic Church', with especial mention of the Pope and the Bishop. In fact the circle is extended beyond the limits of the earth to include the Church Triumphant with which we form one *communio*—one community—as we are reminded just before the consecration.

Nevertheless at each individual celebration of the Mass there stands in the foreground the particular community which here and now is gathered about the celebrating priest. That is very clearly expressed in the liturgy of the Mass. The priest speaks in the plural not as the spokesman of any indeterminate group of people or even as the spokesman of the entire Church. Before many of the prayers he explicitly calls on the community which is here and now gathered together to join him in communal prayer: *Oremus*, 'Let us pray'. He even turns round and speaks to or at them, not with any vague general announcement as though to say 'My brothers and sisters we shall now pray', but he extends to them a specific greeting; a greeting, moreover, which they are expected to answer. Even that does not suffice: it is envisaged that at the end of the prayer all those present should cry out *Amen*.

And when he comes to the very sacrificial prayer, the

eucharistic prayer, the priest expresses his invitations even more emphatically. He says *Sursum corda*, and follows with *Gratias agamus*. And at that point where, in all forms of the liturgy, there is stated in the most solemn manner precisely what is happening here at the altar—where the 'calling to mind' and offering of sacrifice are formulated in words—at that point there is named as agent not only the holder of the priestly office but also the 'holy people'—*nos servi tui sed et plebs sancta tua*. In addition to all this we have the fact that the development of the Mass-rite went still further: it ensured an unmistakable indication that the sacrifice was being offered, within the totality of the Church, precisely by those members of it here and now gathered about the priest. This was effected by the Offertory procession which flourished for more than a thousand years in the Western Church, and of which a trace remains even today in the form of the Offertory verse. The procession expressed very clearly: this is our sacrifice which we are offering. It begins with the bread from our fields and the wine from our vineyards, involving the daily work of our hands and all that goes to make up our lives. This was no mere general consideration or symbol of the common inclusion of earthly life, but more specifically that this community, these people who are now assembled, Sunday by Sunday are to bring their loaves of bread and flasks of wine to the altar in order that their gifts may be consecrated into the sacrificial gift of Christ and offered to God.

That the assembled faithful are all invited to Communion within the Mass in direct connection with their sacrifice follows naturally from what has been described. Nowadays in every country this is an accepted consequence recognised in practice.

The consequence of intrinsic connection has been emphasised by the expressed wish of our Holy Father that whenever possible the faithful should be given Communion from hosts consecrated at that same Mass, as 'a share of that same sacrifice of which they also—in their own way—are the Offerers'. (*Mediator Dei*, n. 126.)* It would be difficult to find a more explicit manner of stating that the Mass is the sacrifice of the *Church*; not merely of the Church as a whole, but primarily and immediately of that community now gathered together.

This is a very sublime thought, and we cannot be surprised that there have been in the past generations of men who reacted to it with a kind of holy awe—generations who cried out with Simon Peter: 'Depart from me, O Lord, for I am a sinful man!' (Luke 5, 8.) The Middle Ages came more and more to adopt this attitude. The people of those days were not only afraid to receive Holy Communion frequently, (three times a year, and later on only once a year, was the normal practice of even good Christians) but they recoiled from the thought that the ordinary faithful should be able to offer the sacrifice with the priest, even with Christ himself. Indeed this was not explicitly denied, but the thought was never exploited pastorally. The whole spiritual and theological atmosphere

*Unless otherwise indicated, quotations from encyclicals are from the English Catholic Truth Society editions.

was such that, especially since the eighth century, an ever increasing emphasis was placed on the dividing line between clergy and people. An invisible wall was built up between the people and the altar.

There was then no clear understanding of the distinct concepts of offering sacrifice and of consecrating. Hence there was a fear that any mention of the faithful as co-offerers of the sacrifice might be misunderstood to imply that they were co-consecrators. In the old Roman Canon of the Mass it was said of the *circumstantes* plainly and simply: *qui tibi offerunt hoc sacrificium laudis*, 'who offer to thee this sacrifice of praise'. But now this phrase was amplified by the insertion of qualifying words so that it became: *pro quibus tibi offerimus vel qui tibi offerunt* . . . 'for whom we offer, or who themselves offer . . .'. The Church of our own day has overcome this bashfulness. It is not a matter of any change in doctrine, but only of a change in attitude—of consequences that may follow or not follow in practice. We have no less reason for being conscious of our spiritual poverty than had the men of the Middle Ages; but we seem more conscious and grateful (as we should be) that we have been redeemed, purified and healed by the Blood of Christ. Pius X invited the faithful to approach the Table of the Lord even daily; for if we are children of God then it is lawful for us to eat the Bread of God's Children. And Pius XII has now declared explicitly that 'the people's offering of the sacrifice pertains to liturgical worship'. And the same Pius has adopted as his own the words of his predecessor Pius XI concerning the *actuosa participatio*, the active participation of the faithful in the liturgy of the Church.[4] But in what does this active participation consist? Only in praying and singing? That the faithful are called on to pray together and sing together is easily understood. But much more is involved.

Already in the encyclical *Mystici Corporis* of 1943 the thought finds expression. In that part where the eucharistic sacrifice is discussed we find: 'The sacred ministers represent not only our Saviour but also the whole Mystical Body and each one of its members; in that sacrifice the faithful are associated in the common prayer and supplication and, through the hands of the priest, whose voice alone renders the Immaculate Lamb present on the altar, they themselves offer to the Eternal Father this most pleasing Victim of praise and propitiation for the needs of the whole Church'.[5]

The Holy Father treats of this matter more at length in his encyclical on the Sacred Liturgy, *Mediator Dei*, of 1947. He begins from the teaching that the faithful in Baptism, by reason of their baptismal character, are appointed to the worship of God and therefore have a share, according to their status, in the priesthood of Christ. Then he gives a more detailed explanation: 'The unbloody immolation by which, after the words of consecration have been pronounced, Christ is rendered present on the altar in the state of victim, is performed by the priest alone, and by the priest in so far as he acts in the name of Christ, not in so far as he represents the faithful. But the

4 *Mediator Dei*, n. 203, quoting Pius XI. Const. *Divini cultus* 1928.

5 *Mystici Corporis*, n. 81.

priest, by the very act of placing the divine victim on the altar, thereby offers it to God the Father as an oblation for the glory of the Blessed Trinity and for the benefit of the whole Church. This offering, understood in the restricted sense of the word, is shared by the faithful, after their own fashion, in a twofold way: for they offer the sacrifice not only through the hands of the priest, but also, in a certain sense, with him. And it is by reason of this participation that the offering by the people is also included in liturgical worship.'[6]

Now follow some further reasons: 'That the faithful offer the sacrifice through the priest is clear from the fact that the minister at the altar acts in the person of Christ considered as Head, and as offering in the name of all the members; and this is why it is true to say that the whole Church makes the offering of the victim through Christ.' And later the Pope adds: 'We rejoice to know that this doctrine has been brought into prominence, especially in recent times, through a more intensive and widespread study of the liturgy.'[7] But he warns that we must be careful not to draw from it unwarranted conclusions, such as that Masses celebrated without any participation of the people would be invalid or unjustifiable.

The Mass is, then, the sacrifice of the Church and, indeed, of that congregation of the faithful here and now gathered about the priest. That is why they may read in their missals the prayers of the priest.

For that reason it is right that they should make the ans-

6 *Mediator Dei*. Translated from A.A.S. 39 (1947) 555-556.

7 *Mediator Dei*, nn. 96, 97, 99.

wers to the priest's prayers, and join in with him in saying aloud the *Gloria*, *Credo*, *Sanctus* and so forth as happens in Dialogue Mass. For that reason they should be aware that the priest says the great *Offerimus* after the consecration in their name. It is clear that only in this way can the concept of the Church become really alive in the minds of the faithful, and that the liturgy can effectively exert its great power to renew pastoral work. 'The Church' is thus no more a merely nebulous idea referring only to the Pope, bishops and priests as responsible for the salvation of our souls. The Church means ourselves; the Church means 'God's holy people', the community of the redeemed, those who have been incorporated into the holy unity of the Body of Christ, who can thus glorify God *per Christum Dominum nostrum*, and who with him can offer the great sacrifice by which his name is glorified from the rising of the sun even until the going down thereof.

It is only to be expected that a community not hitherto accustomed to these things cannot suddenly take to all the various Mass-forms fostered by the liturgical movement, with Dialogue Mass, Offertory procession, Gregorian chant and all the other things which are new to them. A slow preparation is needed and a gradual introduction; and it must consist not merely in an explanation of the new forms but above all a familiarisation with the basic considerations which underlie these things. Even an explanation of the Mass in the spirit of the liturgical movement is insufficient; it is necessary to go deeper than that, into the true concept of the Church. The Church must be grasped as the community of those who belong to Christ and have a part in his life, as the Flock of the Good Shepherd, as the Temple of God built up of living stones, as the Mystical Body of Christ so fully explained in the encyclical *Mystici Corporis*.

Only then will the people grasp and become joyously conscious of how closely we are united to Christ, how we can pray with him and offer sacrifice with him. Then it will come about that the more perceptive members of the community will of themselves voice the desire that these truths should be given expression in the very form of divine service. When that point has been reached it is time to introduce the community step by step into the various ways of active participation and to educate them still further.

On the other hand it is also clear that the ways in which the communal praying and offering of the faithful are given expression will themselves exert a beneficent influence on the grasp which the people have on their faith, provided, of course, that these methods are kept living and meaningful by the whole technique of pastoral work, and not allowed to harden into mere empty mechanical activity. When all of them together cry out the *Kyrie*, when all together, in union with the angels of heaven, sing the *Sanctus*, when all together kneel at the Table of the Lord to receive the Bread of Heaven, then all must consciously feel what a holy community the Church is, and that through the Church we already belong to a higher world even though we still dwell on this poor earth.

In this manner the people can learn ever anew and more deeply all that Christ means to us, that he is truly 'the Mediator between God and man' (1 Tim. 2, 5), through whom alone we can find our way to God. They will grasp and experience what God is—the great and holy God. They learn to adore God and to glorify him. They learn to break free from their small selves. They can realise what divine service truly is: 'It is good to give thanks to the Lord, and to sing to thy name, O most High, to declare thy goodness' (Ps. 91, 1, 2), and the Sunday Mass can become a mighty force impelling them to serve God and remain true to him in their daily lives.

If these convictions are made living, then the spirit of gratitude will be awakened and strengthened—that basic Christian attitude from which the form of our Mass-liturgy, the *eucharistia*, took its origin. All those who have learned to celebrate Mass together and to think together the thoughts of the Mass will feel the *Gratias agamus* as the fulfilment of a need of their thankful souls—still more of a need common to the whole Church filled with gratitude. They will appreciate with a new joy the great festal Prefaces in which the heritage of the ancient Church lives on: thanks to God that Mary, in the immaculate splendour of virginity, gave to us the Light of the world; that the only-begotten Son of God appeared in the form of our mortal flesh; that God has wrought the salvation of mankind on the wood of the Cross; that Christ by dying has brought our death to naught, and by rising again has restored us to life.

And so the Mass, and the liturgy of the Mass when effectively celebrated, will exercise a tremendous educative and uplifting influence upon the faithful.

The eucharistic celebration is, however, not only a *eucharistia* in words, but also a thanksgiving in action, in co-action and co-offering with Christ. In the Mass we are to do homage to Almighty God through a gift which we present to him in reverence, through a sacrificial offering after the manner of all peoples throughout all time. But what sort of a gift is this to be?

It is obvious that in the case of Christians this must be an especially choice and noble gift; it cannot be the blood of goats or heifers or the hecatombs of ancient pagan religions. Yet why should it not be a gift of wine poured forth as a libation in holy places, or sacred fire nourished with precious woods, or the gift of incense to be consumed in the glowing charcoal and wafted aloft in sweet fragrance?

Christ our Lord desired that his brethren should offer a sacrifice no less worthy than that which he himself had offered to his heavenly Father, and he wanted them to be able to offer it with him. He summons us day by day up on to his holy mountain where he wishes to pray no longer alone as he once did during the quiet nights in Palestine. And so now he puts his very own sacrifice into our trembling hands that with him we may offer it, and none other, to his Father.

But why, day by day, must it be such a great and heavenly gift that we can hardly bear it in our hands? Sacrifice is an expression of interior dispositions. Without corresponding dispositions it would be but falsehood. Whoever offers a sacrifice to God is saying thereby at least that he worships God as the most high Lord and intends to observe his law. But is that sufficient for a Christian who offers sacrifice? From a Christian yet more is expected, and that is why his sacrificial gift must be of a higher type. He has been told: 'Be ye perfect as your heavenly Father is perfect' (Matt. 5, 48), and yet again: 'Love one another as I have loved you' (John 13, 34). It is expected of the Christian that he should ever more and more form in himself those dispositions which inspired, and still ever inspire, his Master. That is why St Paul exhorts us: 'Let this mind be in you which was also in Christ Jesus' (Phil. 2, 5), and goes on to sketch for us the picture of the Son of God who emptied himself, taking the form of a servant, becoming obedient even unto the death of the Cross. This is the picture which every Mass holds up before our eyes: that of the Saviour who gives his all to glorify his Father, and does this in merciful love for men, to save them even in the very instant when they reject him.

That we may gradually come to learn all this from him Christ invites us daily to offer his sacrifice with him. Here is truly fulfilled the likeness of the eagle which carries its young aloft on its own back that they may learn to fly (Deut. 32, 11). At first the little ones had no courage to make the attempt; they felt safer and better hidden in their warm nest. But finally they were caught up in the flight of their mother and dared themselves to soar into the sunlight. In like manner, in the hearts of the faithful there will surely one day be ignited that fire which ever glows in the heart of the God-man; or rather, this fire must be enkindled each day in order that we may not grow weary amid the trials of everyday life.

Such thoughts are not new: often they have been expressed in connection with Holy Communion. But there is a difference according to whether we foster and savour them from the point of view of Communion and thus in a kind of isolation, or whether we embrace them in the perspective of the whole eucharistic celebration. It is not here a question of a quiet abiding with Christ which is to expand in thought to the exigencies and duties of Christian ascetics, but rather of the totality and summit of Christian life itself. It has to do with the co-praying and co-offering of the Church and of the individual Christian with Christ. It concerns the sacramentally dedicated self-giving to the will of God along the path of the passion and death which Christ has traversed before us and in which he still precedes us, and thus with a self-abandonment as unreserved and unremitting as that which Christ put into his own sacrifice.

In this way the Mass becomes a school of perfection in which the Christian learns the mind and heart of Christ, or, as St Augustine expresses it: 'in which the Church learns to offer herself'.[8]

The liturgy of Holy Mass is an exceedingly ancient structure. At first sight much of it looks very strange because it derives from an age long past. But it would be a great pity if we, with a kind of bourgeois modesty, were

8 St Augustine, *De civitate Dei*, 10, 20 . . . *'se ipsam per ipsum discit offerre'*.

content to live in a mere corner of this sublime castle. No; this is the Temple of God, here are vast halls in which the people of God can be assembled, including the people of today. This is the Mountain of the Lord of which Isaias spoke, telling the people to climb up: 'Come, let us go up to the mountain of the Lord, and to the house of the God of Jacob. He will teach us his ways and we will walk in his paths.' (Is. 2, 3.) Here must the Father find those adorers whom he seeks, here must we learn from the Son himself to glorify God and 'to adore the Father in spirit and in truth' (John 4, 23).

II

THE CELEBRATION OF SUNDAY AND THE LIFE OF THE CHURCH

THE restoration of Sunday and of the Sunday Mass to full effectiveness is a task so great that a glance into history is truly worth while. Looking back will help us to see how former ages regarded this task, and in what manner and with what success it was accomplished.

We are not thinking here of the question of going back to old forms and old methods; our times are now different, and the problem must be viewed apart from the circumstances of any particular age. But it cannot fail to be useful to us if we try to see and to feel the hidden power that is latent in the Sunday by a study of the example and the success of former generations in using it; we shall thus know what we are to elicit from it and render ever more fruitful for our own times. For this purpose we shall direct our attention chiefly to the heyday of the Church's development, especially to the time of transition from Christian antiquity which was the foundation of the Christian culture of the Middle Ages.

First of all we must disengage the essential idea of the Sunday as it was viewed by the men of those times. This will help us to grasp the meaning of the Sunday Mass as viewed from the standpoint of that period.

The Sunday is not the continuation of the Sabbath in the sense that, following the example of Old Testament practice, the men of those days wanted to set apart one specially holy day each week, but desired to choose for this purpose a different day. The idea of a 'day of rest', which underlay the Jewish practice, was completely absent from the Christian celebration. In fact they even used to poke fun at the Jews for spending a whole day in idleness every week. Many centuries were to pass before it occurred to anyone to connect up the Christian Sunday with the Third Commandment. This commandment was interpreted allegorically in terms of the Sabbath rest of the spirit which Christians were observing all the while, or else of the Sabbath rest of eternal life towards which they were ever striving. The only relic of old Testament tradition which was taken over by the Christians in connection with Sunday was the practice of reckoning time in seven-day periods, or weeks. This was naturally preserved amongst them because it obtained throughout the Greco-Roman world at the time when Christianity began to spread.

A basic idea which underlay the Christian weekly Sunday was the same as that of the yearly Easter—namely, to keep vivid the consciousness that we have been redeemed by Christ. According to the outlook prevalent amongst us today we might have expected that for this purpose choice would have fallen on Friday as being the day on which Christ died upon the Cross. But early Christians did not analyse into constituents the various phases of the work of our redemption; they regarded the redemption as one dramatic occurrence, as one great battle which Christ had fought for the salvation of mankind, as the struggle in which he seemed at first to be conquered, but then emerged clearly as the victor in his resurrection. Christ was viewed as having gone before us through all the humiliations and miseries of this earthly life, as having preceded us through suffering and death, only to show us that this way leads to the light and glory of God the Father.

Hence Sunday is the day of triumph, of exultation and of certain hope for all Christians. It is the day of new creation. That is why, as early as the second century, it was frequently called the 'Eighth Day'. For in six days God had accomplished the first creation; on the seventh day, the Sabbath, he had rested from his work; but on the eighth day, Sunday, he had resumed his work and brought it most wondrously to completion in the resurrection of Christ by which there has been opened to us the way to the everlasting Kingdom of God (*aeternitatis nobis aditum devicta morte reserasti*). Thus the day which, according to the Jewish nomenclature still current at the beginning of Christian times, was called *una sabbati*, the first day of the week, soon had its name changed. Christian speech transposed it from the beginning of the week to the end and called it the Eighth Day—even though in another sense it was still thought of as the 'First Day', the day of the new beginning. But from this time 'eight' became, in the numerical symbolism of the patristic writings, the number which stood for perfection or completion; *octava summa virtutum est*, 'eight is the sum-total, the essence of all virtues', we read in the lesson by St Ambrose in the Breviary.

But the name which was most characteristically attached to this day throughout the whole Greek-speaking and Latin-speaking domains of Christendom was *Kyriake, Dominica*, 'The Lord's Day'. And this name, already used in the Apocalypse of St John, indicates what was in the minds of the Christians who used it; it did not mean the day of the 'Lord' in the Old Testament sense, the day of God and of his dominion; it meant rather the day of resurrection, on which (as St Peter said) 'God hath made both Lord and Christ this Jesus who was crucified' (Acts 2, 36). *Kýrion kaì Christòn*: hence *Kyriaké-Dominica.* To the early Christian the word would imply more or less what we would derive if we said 'Christ's Day'. In German-speaking countries it became 'Sonntag', and in English 'Sunday' only because from the earliest times Christians had learned to think of the sun as a symbol of Christ, and of sunrise as a symbol of the resurrection. The Son of God had, in his death (it was considered) gone down into the world of the dead, but in his resurrection he had risen again just as the glorious sun rises once more to a new day.

Therefore Sunday was the day which was devoted to the memory of Christ and of his work of redemption. It was the day on which the Christian was reminded of that unseen world of which he was an inhabitant. It was not just a kind of psychological remembrance, a mere thinking of great events in the past; on the contrary, there was the mysterious rite which Christ himself had founded and left behind to his Church to be done in memory of himself, namely, the celebration of the Eucharist, the Mass.

It belongs essentially to the celebration of Mass to be a rite of remembrance; it is, in fact, a remembrance of those very things commemorated by the Sunday, namely, the work of redemption which had been effected through the passion, death, resurrection and ascension of Christ. This is precisely what is indicated in the Anamnesis, or prayer after the Consecration: *Unde et memores . . . tam beatae passionis nec non et ab inferis resurrectionis sed et in coelos gloriosae ascensionis.* In some such way—whether more succinctly or more at length—begins the prayer after the Consecration in all the various liturgies; there is a statement that we are doing this in memory of the redemption. The work of redemption is made present to us anew, not only in the *plebs sancta*, in God's holy people here gathered together, but even more so in Christ himself who is present sacramentally in the symbols of his passion as *Pascha nostrum*, our Pasch once sacrificed and now again our sacrificial gift to the Father. For, while we call to mind his own sacrifice, we may go a step further and not only make it present again but also accomplish it as our very own: *Unde et memores . . . offerimus.* So, 'remembering, we offer'.

Sunday and the Eucharist, then, belong closely together. The Mass is explicitly designed for the Sunday and the Sunday has its meaning fully expressed only through the Mass; the Mass, in fact, has a paschal-dominical character. It is only secondarily transferable (and has in fact been transferred) to other occasions.

For the Christian of early times the renewal every

Sunday of the *memoria passionis* must have been the fulfilment of a self-evident need. In those days we find no trace of any commandment to go to Mass on Sunday, only plentiful evidence that in point of fact all who dwelt in the town or country did actually assemble for Mass. In the Diocletian persecution the martyrs of Abitene asserted: 'Without the *dominicum* we cannot live'. It is only in the fourth century, at the Synod of Elvira in Spain, that we meet for the first time any formulation of a Sunday duty: If anyone lives in the town and yet does not come to Mass for three Sundays, he is to be punished by being denied admission to the Mass for some time.

Yet it was by no means easy for the Christians of early times to assemble for Mass on Sundays; they were surrounded by an economic life which knew nothing of any Christian Sunday. Most of them were in positions of dependence, to say nothing of those who were actually slaves. Thus we find that they used to hold their assemblies in the very early mornings, towards dawn: *stato die ante lucem*, as Pliny, the pagan magistrate, averred in his trial of the Christians. Tertullian also speaks of *coetus antelucani* at which the Mass was celebrated. So it was in the last hours of darkness, before the day's work began, that the Christians observed their Sunday.

But with the Peace of the Church, under Constantine in the year 313 A.D., conditions changed very quickly. From various pieces of evidence we know that the time of the Sunday service was changed to the hour at which it was normal to transact really important business, that is, at the 'third hour of the morning'. Soldiers were to be off duty at this hour, that they might attend divine service. Eusebius relates: 'He granted time and opportunity to those soldiers who had embraced the divine faith to go without hindrance to the church, there to offer their prayers undisturbed by anyone.' A little later, until the end of the century, we have explicit information from Egypt and Gaul (the most remote parts of Christendom) that people went every Sunday to Mass and Communion at the third hour. And thus it remained for something like a thousand years.

It remained thus, in fact, as long as it was expected or laid down that all the faithful were to assemble at one single public divine service of the entire Christian community, each to the one single Mass in his own parish. It was not until about the fourteenth century that it became the accepted practice for anyone to go when and where he desired to take part in a Mass. The change of attitude resulted from the abrogation of various rules since the end of the Middle Ages, and from the increasing importance given to the claims of individuals. In the fateful year of 1517 A.D. this state of affairs was first recognised by papal decree.

Until that time, and even to some extent in later days, the Sunday was regarded as the day for a plenary meeting of the Christian community. The Sunday Mass was the occasion at which the Church became visible precisely as a Church, at which the Church manifestly realised itself as an assembly met together in memory of its Lord. Till the sixth century the Sunday was basically nothing other than that. For, until that time, abstention from work was connected with Sunday only in so far as this provided time to be dedicated to divine service. In the laws promulgated by the last few Roman emperors the sanctity of the Sunday was protected by the prohibition of all business in the law courts and of noisy functions such as public circuses and the like; also of noisy forms of trading—seemingly in so far as these would disturb the sanctification of the Sunday. By contrast the prohibition of all Sunday work came into force in the west only during the sixth century; this was brought about partly through suggestion from the now Christianised German races, and partly from the adoption of pertinent regulations taken over from the Old Testament.

But the emphasis remained for a very long time on the requirement of one communal service. The Church became on Sunday visible and tangible as a Church. This was both established and stressed by the very style of the service, for this was communal in nature through and through.

The facts are well known; they are even now to be discerned in our contemporary liturgy which took its definite shape in just this period at the end of Christian antiquity, crystallising in itself authentic earlier traditions. We are not so much thinking of the great Stational Services of the Roman Church and of other bishoprics, where a whole city came together for divine service; for these services were specially solemn forms carried out preferably in immense basilicas. We are thinking rather of the ordinary Sunday Mass.

It was for this that the Christian people in any large city, such as Rome, were from a very early date (even before the end of the persecutions) divided up into smaller communities, each with its own church. As early as the fourth century there were in Rome no less than twenty-five titular churches. These were churches of comparatively small size, in which the voices of the celebrant, deacon, reader and cantor could easily be heard. The language was intelligible to everyone. We have evidence that in Rome itself, as was the case in the earliest times, wherever the Greek-speaking element predominated the liturgy was held in Greek. But since the third century, when the Latin-speaking section gained the ascendancy, there was a change to a Latin liturgy. This happened gradually, so that for a long time a Greek service was held for Greek-speakers, while a Latin service was held for Latin-speakers.

The celebrating priest spoke always in the plural. He prayed in the name of all. He summarised the petitions of all, such as those which had been expressed in the *Kyrie*-litany, into one prayer which he presented before the Throne of God. This prayer of his began with the invitation *Oremus*; and was preceded by his greeting, *Dominus vobiscum*, which was answered by all. This shows the importance attached to union between people and altar.

Before the eucharistic prayer the greeting and invitation were even more emphatic; the greeting is followed by *Sursum corda*, and the invitation takes the form of *Eucharistomen, Gratias agamus*, precisely because it was to lead into the thanksgiving prayer. At the *Sanctus* the entire community joined in. Even well on into the Middle Ages the *Sanctus* was not regarded as an item on its own, to be entrusted to trained singers; for it was a more simple, and thereby more impressive, song of all the people; the community just joined in the easy melody of the preface and sang together with the priest 'and all the heavenly army' the triple *Sanctus*.

Even though this singing was of the simplest, the impression made by such united prayer must have been very powerful. Without any conscious reflection on the form of the liturgy everyone must have felt (merely by hearing and seeing): 'we are fellow-citizens of the angels in heaven'. At the end of the eucharistic prayer, when the consecrated gifts lay upon the altar, when the offering to the Divine Majesty had been expressed and the mighty prayer brought to its conclusions with *Per ipsum et cum ipso et in ipso*, the entire community voiced its assent in the *Amen*. St Jerome recounts how, in the Roman basilicas, this *Amen* used to resound like a thunder-clap.

In addition we must remember that the faithful had a perfectly clear knowledge of what they were assenting to in their *Dignum et justum est* and their *Amen*. It was no mere vague idea amounting just to the knowledge that consecration took place and sacrifice was offered. They knew the exact content of this Sunday prayer of thanks-giving.

From the early Middle Ages there have come down to us a whole series of prefaces which set forth in most impressive language all the chief mysteries of our redemption. God is thanked for having sent us his Son; for having enabled earth-born man to be born again into a life destined for heaven; for the fact that we may be called a chosen race and a kingly priesthood; for the opening to us by Christ of the gates of heaven. Hence the Sunday Mass became in very truth, and subjectively, an expression of conscious gratefulness to God for all that we have received through Christ. This remembering and thanking was spread out over all the great feasts of the Church's year, wherein every important element in the work of our redemption was brought up in turn for consideration: the Incarnation, the saving passion, the outpouring of the Holy Ghost—all these were presented in great word-pictures to the comprehension of every Christian.

The liturgy was a powerful force for instruction and religious training; this aspect came to the fore especially in the readings. The general idea of the Sunday offering of thanks to God was reinforced by the story, from some evangelist, of the suffering or the resurrection of Christ. We have information on this point both from Jerusalem and from the Church of southern Gaul in the sixth century. But those Sunday readings had a further purpose. Even today the Epistles of the Sundays after Easter take us through the 'Catholic Epistles' in turn; and those of the Sundays after Pentecost likewise lead us through the Epistles of St Paul beginning with that to the Romans and ending with the Epistles of the Captivity. In the Greek Byzantine liturgy even the Gospel readings were (and still are) arranged on a similar principle; from the Sundays after Easter onwards we find a more or less continuous series of readings from St John, then another series from St Matthew and finally a series from St Luke. Therefore in the Sunday Mass it was (and still is) the New Testament which occupies the foreground. This corresponds absolutely with the fundamental idea of Sunday and of the Sunday service which is precisely to keep alive in Christian consciousness the fact of the 'New Creation'. There are some liturgies, such as the Egyptian, which use nothing except New Testament readings (and four of them at that) within the Mass. With us there are some Old Testament readings in use, but these are always on days which are not Sundays.

Even so, the faithful of the early Church must have been quite familiar with the Old Testament, at least as regards certain extracts which were regarded and used as fore-types of the New Testament, and especially as regards certain figures which were types of Christ or of the Church or of the sacraments. This familiarity came to the faithful of old chiefly through readings within the liturgy. For it is striking that among those pictures which were favourites with the people—such as those found in the catacombs and on sarcophagi dating from the fourth and fifth centuries—there keep on recurring such typical scenes as the following: Noe who was saved from the waters of the flood; Isaac who was sacrificed and yet continued to live: Moses who brought forth water from the rock; Jonas who was cast into the sea and yet was saved; the three young men who came forth alive from their fiery tomb, and so on. Behind all this familiarity it is clear that there stands a series of liturgical readings. These are chiefly the readings of the great Vigils from Saturday to Sunday of the Ember Days, and those of the Easter Vigil. The prophecies of Holy Saturday bring before us even today the majority of these figures; and the readings about the three young men in the fiery furnace still occur on each Ember Saturday.

But even in the ordinary Sunday service there was some place available for the use of Holy Scripture from the Old Testament. From the sphere of the Greek liturgies —especially from Cappadocia and Cyprus—we have information that on Saturdays and Sundays at Vespers it was the regular practice to read the Bible to the people. Even in the West there must have been a good deal of Bible-reading in church. Caesarius of Arles gives us many indications of this practice. Augustine, in his Confessions, tells us of his mother Monica that regularly, twice a day, *mane et vespere*, she went to church to pray and to hear the Word of God—*ut te audiat in tuis sermonibus, et tu illam in suis orationibus*. Even though this refers to the customs of an African town (it seems to have been Tagaste), we gather that it was usual, both in the morning and the evening (that is, at matins and vespers), to have scripture readings every day. This would have been true of other centres, at least on Sundays; scripture was read in the Hours to which the people came (especially Vespers) at those points where we find, even today, a *Capitulum*.

There was also another way in which the eucharistic

Sunday service did much to make the people familiar with Holy Scripture. This was in the psalmody, especially that which occurred in between the scripture readings. We cannot assume that the people knew by heart any great number of psalms. They would know only those which were in constant use at the Hours which they themselves frequented, that is, at Lauds and Vespers. They would thus know some morning psalms and some evening psalms. Thus we find that Caesarius of Arles takes it for granted that everyone would know Psalm 90 (*Qui habitat*) by heart. When mentioning an extract from the Psalm of Nature (Psalm 103), *Sol cognovit occasum suum*, he likewise remarks that this would be so familiar throughout the world that the majority of Christians would know it by heart.

But above all certain verses of the psalms must have become, as it were, almost part of the flesh and blood of the people through their constant use at the Sunday Mass. Up till the fifth century there was only one place in the Mass where there was any question of artistic singing—that which occurred between the readings (our Gradual and *Alleluia*). At that point one of the singers, known as the *Psalmista* (Cantor), went up into the Ambo, and there sang one single verse, or even phrase, of some psalm; for example, at Easter, *Haec dies quam fecit Dominus exultemus et laetemur in ea*. The people immediately repeated this verse. The choir then began with the first verse of the psalm, after which the people repeated their chorus, *Haec dies*, doing the same after all subsequent verses. From Augustine we learn more details about the practice, in the western Church, of this so-called responsorial singing. It was the celebrant (bishop or priest) who chose which psalm and which responsory should be used on any occasion. Obviously he would choose each time some verse which had an apt and meaningful content: *Venite exultemus Domino*; *Exaltabo te Domine, quoniam suscepisti me*; or something in the nature of a petition such as: *Ne perdas cum impiis animam meam.* Most frequently it was the cry of joy, *Alleluia*, which even now remains in almost daily use with some psalm-verse before the Gospel. This verse, sung to some simple melody, must have sunk deep into the minds and hearts of the people. Here was a school of prayer, more especially of the prayer of adoration and praise, which was effective to a degree not to be under-estimated.

Thus the Sunday Mass, for the Christians of the early Church, was not merely 'Divine Service' (and, indeed a very worthy and dignified Divine Service), but it was also, in its secondary aspects, a school of prayer and a school of instruction. And this can be said not only of the words of the official prayers, but also of the communal actions which were of considerable importance.

Among these must be reckoned joining in the responses and the singing, observance of the communal order of standing, kneeling, stretching out the hands in the 'Orante position', the sharing of all, by Communion, in the 'one Bread', and especially the Offertory procession. This procession was the obvious counterpart to the Communion procession.

The Offertory procession had, moreover, a most important didactic function. For, by contrast with the heathen religions, the Church of early centuries laid great emphasis on the spiritual nature of its divine service; true worship consisted not in the offering of tremendous material gifts or externally impressive celebrations, but rather in service of the heart, in worship 'in spirit and in truth', an *oblatio rationabilis*. But, on the periphery of the Christian community, there were to be found the protagonists of 'enlightened Christianity', the Gnostics. These had seized on the spiritual nature of worship, but had exaggerated the idea into a still more 'spiritualised' view which amounted to heresy; they were so 'spiritual' that they repudiated all the visible elements of the Church. Gnosticism professed a Christianity in which everything external or material was deemed to be worthless; the material world was regarded as evil in itself, the work of the devil. The Church, therefore, was obliged to undertake the defence of material creation. She began, therefore, to bring into prominence the material gifts in which the Christian sacrifice finds its beginning, as though to say: The spiritual nature of our sacrifice is not to be understood in the sense that it does not originate in the gifts which come from this earth, and which are the fruits of our daily toil and a symbol of our earthly life. And so from this time onwards the Offertory procession in the Mass rite was stressed and amplified. The Offertory procession of the faithful who advanced to the altar bringing their own personal gifts of bread and wine was the liturgical answer which the Church gave to the false teachings of the Gnostics. For in this procession there is expressed the idea that the Divine Service on Sunday does not only honour God and continue the work of Christ, but also it sanctifies earthly life and lifts it up towards God. Even today we have a reminder of the same idea in the word *missa*, Mass. For in the speech idiom of the ancient Church, *missa* meant the same as 'blessing'. The *Missa*, the Mass, is the dedication to God every Sunday—in fact, the blessing—of human life and of the earthly world in which it is lived.

From all this we can obtain some idea of what a formative and transforming power was brought to bear on everyday life, not merely by the observance of Sunday, but, in particular, by the celebration of the Sunday Mass. The light of Christian teaching shone forth in it with brilliance; the 'Memory of the Lord' was made vivid and living; the assembled community must have felt that it was gathered together as the *plebs sancta*, as the visible manifestation of the *Ecclesia*; and that Christ himself was present amongst them—that very Christ whose picture looked down upon them from the scintillating mosaic of the apse. The religious knowledge which was derived from the Sunday Mass was, as someone strikingly expressed it, a by-product of simply living with the Church. Just as a child, by living with its mother day by day, picks up its mother's speech and grows into its mother's outlook, so did the faithful grow up in the speech and thought and mind of the Church by uttering her prayers together and celebrating her Divine Service.

It is possible, however, to voice a doubt concerning this

picture which we have drawn of the Christian Sunday of early days. May it not be that we have put together various features and details which, in fact, were not found together, but were spread out in different places and times within that period of the Church's life which we are wont to call 'Christian antiquity'? Perhaps in this way we have painted a picture which is too beautiful, and have presented an ideal concept of those times rather than any reality? It is difficult to give any direct answer to this objection, for the sources of information which are at our disposal are indeed scanty, and begin to impart a message to us only when they are put together. That was an age wherein people were not much given to writing about things which they actually lived. We have to fall back on chance remarks, little 'asides' which are to be found in the letters and sermons of the early Fathers, in their occasional writings, in the Acts of the Martyrs, and on inferences from liturgical texts which, for their own part, are often fragmentary.

However, it is already something rather remarkable when a former age has transmitted to us, even in fragments, enough information for us to be able to see vividly the clear ideal of a truly noble divine worship. This would be true if the men of that age had not succeeded (as is so often the case in human affairs) in putting their ideals into practice. But there is much indirect evidence which makes us certain that they did in fact achieve an extremely high standard. For we are in a position of being able to assess what they achieved by examining its results.

To begin with, we can be absolutely certain that in Christian antiquity the Sunday Mass was by far the most important—if not the only—pastoral activity of those days. The Mass was regularly celebrated in public only on Sundays. Feasts of martyrs were celebrated only at the places of their martyrdom, usually at their graves. There were no public Masses on weekdays except for certain days in Lent, and for Ember days. The *Proprium de tempore* of our missal constituted the full programme of the public worship of the Roman Church until well on into the Middle Ages. We do, indeed, find references here and there to a Mass on a weekday; but all these are concerned with celebrations for small groups, for funeral Masses, votive Masses and the like. To the Sunday Masses there can be added, as public liturgical functions on weekdays, nothing but Matins or Lauds in the morning, and Vespers in the evening. And to these came only a small minority of the Christians of any place—just as now such a minority comes to church on weekdays.

Another point to note is that even at Sunday Masses, at least in Rome, there was seldom any sermon. From a decree of Pope Coelestine I we know that simple priests (and therefore the priests of the titular churches in Rome) had no authorisation to preach; the office of preaching was reserved to the bishop. Only in a few particular instances in the western Church (such as those given by Augustine and Caesarius of Arles) was there any exception to this rule.

Other institutions which, according to our present notions, are indispensable elements of normal pastoral practice, just did not exist at all. There was indeed a well-developed charitable activity carried on under the direction of the deacons and ecclesiastical almoners; but charitable work is one of the fruits, rather than one of the methods, of the apostolate. There were no Christian schools—neither elementary nor secondary. Whatever organised schooling was to be found was—certainly until the fourth century—in the hands of pagans. There were no Catechism classes—either in or out of school; children had to be brought up by their parents to Christian doctrine and Christian life. The Church had no kind of 'Youth Movement'; the youth had to find their own way. There was nothing bearing any resemblance to organised Catholic Action. There were not even any missionary institutions, for the purpose of spreading Christianity among the pagans. There were no pious associations or confraternities; the one and only Christian association was the Church herself, and the only meeting of it was the Sunday service.

But always there was the Christian Sunday; and there was on Sunday a liturgy which was truly living, and closely connected with the life and feeling of the people. And the power of its inspiration must have been so overwhelming that it sufficed to stand in the place of all those other things which we are accustomed to regard as indispensable for effective pastoral work; it sufficed to make families so Christian that they succeeded in bringing up Christian children; it sufficed to impregnate Christians with a community-consciousness and a grasp of the true nature of the Church; it sufficed to inspire the faithful (or at least a sufficient number of them) with a spirit so apostolic that they could and did win the pagans to Christ.

For the very period of history in which all the above features were missing was the period in which Christianity triumphed over paganism. It triumphed not only exteriorly but also interiorly, in that it brought about that fundamental transformation whereby a pagan society became a Christian society, a pagan world became a Christian world; it was that period in which was effected a complete revolution in contemporary thought by the shift of emphasis from the world of time to the world of eternity, and by a new evaluation of human life, of the position of women, of slaves and of children (even unborn children) in human society. In short, this period saw the pagan philosophy of life superseded by a Christian philosophy which finally blossomed forth into the Christian culture of the Middle Ages. And when we look for visible and human factors to which we can ascribe this amazing transformation, we can find none other than the liturgy of the Church, especially the Sunday Mass-liturgy.

From this we do not argue that we should now, in this twentieth century, return to the same way of celebrating Sunday and to the identical Sunday Mass-liturgy which they had in those days. We are not drawing the conclusion that the Sunday Mass should become again the one and only fount of Christian instruction and training. For, after all, we have our Christian schools, our Catechism classes, and all manner of ways for propagating the faith both in the spoken and the written word. We are not arguing that the community of the faithful should find its sole expression in the assembly for one single Sunday Mass. For we have many forms of group-apostolate and organised activity. On the other hand we ought to realise that the social character of the liturgy of the Roman rite which is common to so many countries of the Church Universal, and the venerable tradition which connects us with the early Church, is of enormous value for the Church of today.

For we of the twentieth century are in a paganised world, in a secularised atmosphere which, in spite of all our apostolic endeavours, has penetrated into the midst of our people and has largely de-Christianised them. We are not in so strong a position that we can afford to neglect the great power which could be derived from a living Sunday liturgy, a liturgy suited to the people. The past ten years have opened to us some interesting possibilities. It is for ecclesiastical authority to examine what further advances can be made. It is, however, for all who have the care of souls to make the most effective use of those possibilities which are now at our disposal, and to work with them for the buiding up of the Church and the Christian renewal of the world.

III

COMMUNAL CELEBRATION OF THE MASS IN JEOPARDY

In the course of centuries the one immutable holy sacrifice which Christ entrusted to his Church has undergone a radical change in the manner in which it is also the sacrifice of the Church. In fact one can say that by far the majority of all the changes in the liturgy of the Mass from Peter to Pius XII are to be measured in terms of the manner and the degree in which the Holy Mass is shown forth as the sacrifice of the Church.

The Mass as the Church's sacrifice is above all, as we have already seen, the sacrifice of Christ. And that not only in the sense that he instituted it, and is still the victim of it because his flesh and blood are offered on the altar, but also in the sense that it is he who really and primarily offers it in the person of the ordained priest who stands at the altar, who represents him and who, in his name, pronounces the decisive words.

But the priest also represents the community which offers its sacrifice with him and through him—the same sacrifice which Christ offered in the first instance alone and deserted on Calvary, but now continues to offer on every altar with the intention that his Church is to join herself to him, to enter into his sacrifice and prayer, into his thought and will, into his self-giving to his heavenly Father, so that with him and in him (*cum ipso et in ipso*) united praise may be given to God's unending majesty.

Now if, in the minds of the faithful, the sacrifice of Christ pushes all other aspects into the background, especially that of the co-offering by the Church, the consequence is a danger to the Mass as regards the manner in which it is actually celebrated. The one predominant aspect so overshadows everything else that the rest may degenerate into a merely external basically indifferent setting for the precious jewel. And thus there arise forms of devotion in which the sacrifice of the Church scarcely receives any recognition, even if we have to concede that such forms are both possible and justifiable within the Church. Even the old grandmother who comes to Mass and spends the whole time fingering her rosary, but is happy to be there and to share in the blessings of the Mass in order to go comforted and strengthened to her home; even the silent gathering of individual faithful to be seen in the nave of the church on Sundays while the priest at the altar 'says Mass'; even these do have some share in the sacrifice of the Church although the communal aspect of the sacrifice is practically undiscernible.

We know, however, that in the early days of the Church things were nothing like this. And, in view of a return to a more total view and practice, it may be helpful to investigate the reasons why and the manner in which things became so different. We may discern what influences have been at work, and perhaps are still at work; what obstacles prevented, and perhaps are still preventing, a bodying forth of the concept of the Church in the very worship of the Church; what factors we have to watch if the Mass is ever again to become recognisable in the fullest sense as the sacrifice of the Church.

Firstly there is an adverse influence which was already felt about the latter days of Christian antiquity—namely, *embellishment*.

The Church became great and rich, her basilicas spacious, her clergy numerous. Everything which the culture of those days could offer stood at her disposal. And it was taken into use, at least for the Stational services on great feasts.

We do not know in precise detail how the ordinary parish Mass was conducted in the titular churches and village churches at this period. Probably the changes from the simple practice of the preceding times were but slight. We have precise knowledge only of that type of Mass which gradually became so splendid and complicated that its details had to be written down in the *Ordines Romani*. This was the Stational Mass celebrated by the Pope, at which were present the entire papal court, the Roman nobility and a great many people from every region of the city. Here appears for the first time a specialist choir of singers, the so-called *schola cantorum*.

In the Christian worship of the first centuries there was indeed singing, but a special choir was unknown. The people themselves did the singing, even though in an unpretentious manner. They joined in the *Sanctus* by merely continuing the same recitative-like melody in which the celebrant had begun his Thanksgiving prayer (Preface). The people sang in between the scripture readings, and sang during the Communion. For the rest, no voices were heard except those of the celebrant and of the reader. The people's song between the readings and at the Communion was led by a cantor in what is known as responsorial singing: that is, the cantor first sang to the people a short phrase which they repeated after every verse or every strophe of the psalm.

But some time in the fifth century the Schola made its appearance in the churches. It began to enrich the proceedings by antiphonal singing, two sections in alternation. The Schola sang during the entrance procession of the clergy, during the Offertory procession of the people and also during their Communion procession. There would seem to be no objection to that. It is easy to understand why the people's singing at the Communion was replaced by the antiphonal singing of the Schola; but soon the same thing happened with regard to the singing between the readings. The ancient form of it was indeed kept; it was responsorial singing both in the Gradual and in the *Alleluia*; but the Schola took it over. And it soon became too difficult for the people to be able to join in except in a very imperfect manner. In fact it is very doubtful whether, on festal occasions, the people managed to raise their voices at all, or whether they were even expected to do so.

This development had a most unfavourable effect on subsequent ages in that it was this embellished festal form, which alone was committed to writing, that became spread abroad into other countries as the authentic 'Roman liturgy'. In the Frankish kingdom, long before the days of Charlemagne, the attention of the leading men had been centred on Rome and on the well-ordered Roman liturgy by the aid of which they desired to tidy up the liturgical disorder of their own countries. With zeal and industry they procured liturgical books from Rome, and tried—with or without Roman-trained instructors—to put into practice as best they might whatever they found in these books.

But it was the festal form of Roman liturgy which they thus learned; and it was this which they strove to introduce into their churches as the usual everyday manner of doing things. The complexity of its embellishments obviously made difficulties as regards the active participation of the people and thus was a hindrance to it under its aspect of being the sacrifice of the Church.

There is also a second period in liturgical history when embellishment became very intensive and exercised an influence by no means advantageous on the shaping of divine service; this was the Baroque period. To the utmost limits of available resources the churches were turned into gorgeous 'salons' filled with ostentatious and gaudy decorations in the richest of worldly styles. And the singing was given 'splendour' by the development of polyphonic music; the Mass, in fact, was deliberately turned into 'Grand Opera'. At first this happened only on great occasions or in places which made pretensions to be art centres, that is, in the Court churches and castle chapels. But again there happened a process often exemplified in history, a process which we might call 'the vulgarisation of culture': what was intended as an exceptional form of solemnity little by little became a daily (or at least a weekly) occurrence. And so we find even today in choirs of small parish churches an ambition to 'perform' Sunday by Sunday harmonised Masses which, like a sort of enigmatic tinkling cloud, hover over the congregation and invariably condemn them to silence!

A second danger to the fashioning of a really expressive form for the Church's sacrifice came from a certain obscuring of the *concept of the Church* in the minds of both people and priests since the close of Christian antiquity. This danger was already perceptible even in Carolingian times. It was occasioned by external incidents and circumstances, but still more by those concerned with the history of dogma.

External circumstances had brought about a state of affairs in which the people no longer understood the language used by the priest at the altar. Latin was the speech of distinction, the only written language, the tongue at least moderately well understood by the upper classes among the Franks. The need of change was not felt. In fact the predilection for solemnity even favoured the use of the elegant and rather foreign language. But it led inevitably to a thorough cleavage between the common people and the altar, to a certain hindering of the participation by the people even in an external manner.

But there were also interior influences acting in the same direction. The concept of the Church was no longer so vivid as formerly. Indeed, the faithful knew what the

Church was and who belonged to it; but they did not grasp, as they had done in former days, that the Church was a religious immensity, the community of the redeemed all made one in Christ. Throughout the whole of the Middle Ages the Mystical Body of Christ, so often expounded by St Paul, is rarely discussed in the works of the theologians and spiritual writers of the day. The Church was apprehended principally as a hierarchical structure. It was indeed the same Church which men saw, but from a totally different angle. There became common the viewpoint (of which the aftermath is still with us) that really it is only the Pope, bishops and priests who make up the Church; or at least that these alone have any function in the Church.

This changed outlook upon the Church is easily understood from certain events in the history of dogma which were taking place just about then in the Frankish church, at that time paramount. The piety of the Gallican-Frankish church had developed in the atmosphere of the Christological controversies which, in the fifth and sixth centuries, broke out afresh. They were unleashed by the Arians of German stock, chiefly the west Goths, and raged fiercely for a long time. In consequence of the Arian dangers it became important that the Catholics should be very careful never to speak of Christ in terms which could be taken to imply that in his Godhead he was not of the same nature as the Father. So far as possible they avoided mention even of his Mediatorship.

Consequently the thought of the glorified God-man became somewhat repressed in popular piety. And that meant that the concept of Christ as the living Head of the Church suffered eclipse; this in turn caused the idea of the Church in the popular mind to lose its depth. Inevitably, therefore, the hierarchical structure of the Church came into the foreground, with its stress on the difference between clergy and people; with its tendency also to induce an ever increasing separation between clergy and people, between altar and nave, in divine service. Finally this developed practically into a barrier.

And in point of fact a whole series of symptoms showed that this dividing process had made great headway. At the beginning of the Carolingian period, which started off as a period of religious revival, there were all sorts of attempts to foster the active participation of the people in the Mass. They were supposed to answer the priest, to join in the *Gloria Patri* of the Introit, in the *Sanctus*, and so on. But the atmosphere was not conducive to the success of these attempts. Only the Offertory procession revived to flourish again, but not the Communion. The ninth century saw the end of endeavours to make the course of the Mass, as it really is, intelligible to the people.

Instead it became the fashion to stress the mysterious and unapproachable nature of the sacramental-liturgical action. In Christian antiquity the altar was normally the central point of the half-circle formed by the college of clergy, and was thus near to the people. Now it was pushed into the background against the wall of the apse.

In the greater churches, the cathedral and collegiate churches, the space for the clergy (the choir) was even separated from the space for the people (the nave) by a formal partition (the screen). And behind this there was carried on an avowedly clerical liturgy. Certainly the Christian people were not totally unconcerned with it: by means of rich foundations, naturally of lay provenance, there were instituted colleges of priests or monks who had no other function than to sing God's praises day and night in the Divine Office (which was much longer than it is now), and to perform a Community Mass as the climax of every day. But all this was clerical liturgy.

At public Masses on Sundays and feast days these clergy took over those parts of the Mass which had formerly been sung by the people. For this purpose more elaborate and homogeneous musical compositions were produced —some of them very fine—our 'Plainchant Masses'. (The German word for this is 'Choral', which means 'choir-music'; so the very word, used in this connection, betrays its origin. 'Choir music' is the music to be performed in the choir of the church, by the clergy who occupy the choir-stalls. Later on, in the further developments of the Baroque age, the choir of clergy was in its turn ousted by what we now call the 'church choir'. So the very word 'choir', which once meant practically the same as the clergy in the front of the church, now refers to the laity in the loft at the back of the church.) The people were now silent; and the form of the Mass corresponded with a concept of the Church wherein the laity constituted only a passive element. And this concept was reinforced by what came to pass in Church history during the sixteenth century.

Luther and the Reformers were by no means mistaken in criticising the concept of the Church as it was then manifested in practice. But they did more than criticise: they laid down as their thesis the exact opposite by denying altogether any special priesthood in the Church. All members of the Church were equal: to use Luther's own words, 'Whoever has been fished out of the font can pride himself that he has been ordained priest and bishop and pope!' Hence it became a bitter necessity for the Church, if she were to avoid embarrassment, to emphasise strongly the special priesthood of the ordained clergy, the powers of the priesthood, and the hierarchic organisation of the Church. But obviously this was hardly favourable to the task of activating the laity in the Church!

The authentic doctrine about the nature of the Church has never altered throughout the whole period since the close of Christian antiquity. But within this doctrine the emphasis, as regards the practical life of the Church, has been so placed that the hierarchic aspect has been overstressed and the position of the laity has been understressed. This has revealed itself correspondingly in public worship.

There is a third factor which in recent centuries has worked to the detriment of an effective portrayal of the sacrifice of the Church; and that is *Individualism*. The Individual is to have freedom, and the right to and scope for personal development. The history of culture in general, and of art in particular, establish that this spirit was already making itself felt in the Middle Ages, especially in the late Gothic period: the wonderful orderliness of the Roman period was disintegrating, and classical forms were dissolving into undisciplined ornamentation.

Exactly the same thing is to be observed in the history of the liturgy. Even in the solemn clerical liturgy well-ordered co-operation became impaired. Up till that time the various functionaries—celebrant, lector, schola and choir—had been regarded as contributing with equal rights to the unified action of the whole. On this principle were arranged the different books needed: the sacramentary, the lectionary and the antiphonary. These were part-books for the various roles of those who severally collaborated in the communal action.

But now there came in a rule that the celebrant was to read the entire text including the readings and those parts which were to be sung. He became, after a manner, self-sufficient even in the High Mass. This led to a practical consequence in the realm of books—a consequence which in other respects is not to be deplored. For it led to the compilation of the missal, a book which contains not only the texts of the sacramentary, but also those to be read by the lector and to be sung by the schola and choir; it contains even the rubrics of the Master of Ceremonies taken from the *Ordines*.

Ultimately this turned out to be an advantage in clerical circles. But it was not long before this tendency began to affect the people also. Until the late Middle Ages it was a generally accepted principle that the entire parish should assemble on Sunday for a single communal service. This was the weekly plenary meeting of the community. For this reason it was called at that hour of the day when it was customary to hold important functions or solemn gatherings; this had been done ever since the time of Constantine. The appointed hour was in the middle of the morning, at the 'third hour of the day'. For more than a thousand years this was the fixed rule. For a long time, indeed, there had been such things as private Masses, even on Sundays. But as regards their time and place they had to be arranged so that the people were not admitted to them. Even in the churches of monasteries and convents the Sunday Mass had to be celebrated behind closed doors.

But in the thirteenth century there came changes. The mendicant orders managed to win their battle for the recognition of their own Sunday Masses as having equal rights; and although various Synods passed laws to the contrary, there was finally admitted the principle (acknowledged even by Rome in 1517) that people could fulfil their Sunday obligation by being present at any Mass whatever. Even a private Mass in some place other than the parish church would suffice.

Thus was achieved a momentous break-through for the forces of individualism—or should we rather say for the claims of individuals; for, to be strictly just, we should not regard individualism as an unmixed evil, even in the sphere of divine worship. Now that the exclusiveness of parish rights had been set aside, the way was open for the new active Orders to reach the people by their preaching, to be at their disposal in the confessional, and to do genuine pastoral work which, at that time, was an urgent necessity.

Even in a wider sphere, in the spiritual life in general, individualism (or let us say, more careful regard for persons) has its positive side. Until close on the end of the middle ages, both among regular and secular clergy, the only kind of prayer in general use (apart from spiritual reading) was community prayer, collective prayer—which meant oral prayer. If they wanted to pray still more, then they added some more psalms in choir, or a Votive Office. But in the fifteenth century there arose a kind of movement for personal, meditative prayer. It began in Holland and gradually gained a footing throughout the whole Church. St Ignatius of Loyola adopted this practice of meditation and made it the basis of the Spiritual Exercises, giving it also predominance in his order.

No sincere priest or seminarian of today would dispute the contention that for pastoral work there is need for men of personality; and that such men cannot be developed without the help of personal, that is meditative, prayer. For the laity also personal prayer is a necessity; they must have a certain freedom in the building up of their life of piety; and that applies to their Sundays. In his little book *Das Personliche in der Liturgie* Fr Chrysostom Panfoeder, O.S.B., shows how genuine liturgy, true worship of God, can originate only from the personal prayer of many. Real worship does not consist in the beauty of external forms, but in the sincerity of the common prayer arising from the hearts of the many.

On the other hand we have to assert with conviction that though individualism and the development of what is personal has met with great success in the sphere of culture, the exaggeration of it has produced enormous evils. And in like manner the improvement and gain in the religious sphere has not been attained without losses. When feeling for the Church grows less, then even though the Mass be still loved, appreciation of it as the sacrifice of the Church is diminished, and likewise the taste for communal celebration. The individual becomes absorbed in his prayer-book and carries on his personal devotions.

Of the Middle Ages one can say that communal celebration of the Mass, at least as regards the clergy, had become overdeveloped. By contrast the Low Mass is now the basic form. And this has become so even in official documents of the Church. In the *Missale Romanum* it is the *missa lecta* which is taken as the norm for the *ritus servandus.* In many countries, especially in Ireland and in the United States, Low Mass is the usual form of celebration even on Sundays. In America on a Sunday morning one can see enormous churches packed with people, every place filled, with everything in perfect order and numerous Communions—but no communal singing, no communal praying; the only audible things from beginning to end are perhaps the announcements and the sermon.

There is, however, a beginning of that which has become a powerful movement amongst us here in the last few decades: namely, a slow strengthening of understanding for the true nature of the Church, and with it, a renewal of the communally celebrated Mass as the sacrifice of the Church. The Church is awakening in the souls of the people.

What is needed for this movement to achieve its purpose? We have established three influences which have worked to the detriment of the Mass as the sacrifice of the Church, and of its worthy communal celebration. The only remedy, the only way to remove the shadows in the picture and return to a worthy celebration of divine service, especially in the Mass, is to bring these factors back into proper balance and maintain them so. Let us examine them again, in reverse order.

Individualism. People of today have a right to, and must be allowed to enjoy, a certain liberty. Only in Utopia would it be possible to establish in each parish one single parochial Mass at which all would be present. It is absolutely necessary that there be other Masses at other times. But these ought to be genuine community Masses, so that everyone would be drawn into communal singing and communal praying. But even in these there must be left some opportunity for quiet personal prayer. A suitable form of celebration would be the Dialogue Mass with some carefully chosen hymns incorporated at certain points.

Concepts of the Church. This is even more important; we have to develop and strengthen the concept of the Church. And the way to do this is not to be always speaking of the clergy and of the functions and rights of the hierarchy, or of the Church as a 'perfect society', but rather to foster in the people's minds the consciousness that we all belong to Christ. He is our First-born Brother who has opened for us the way to God our Father. He is our Lord, our King, our Shepherd; he fulfils in our regard all those many roles explained in his parables. We are in him who is our Head; we are his members; all of us together are his Church.

It is, of course, important to teach the faithful about the life on earth of Christ who taught and suffered and offered up his life and died for us; but it is just as important that we should speak to them about the risen Christ, the glorified Christ who continues now, *in the present*, to live and reign (*qui vivit et regnat*), and who, as living Head, unites us all with him in his Church.

It is therefore an enormous gain for the renewal of Catholic life that by the Roman decree of 1951 the Easter Vigil has been restored. For this restoration of the Easter liturgy (which, of course, has to be explained to the people) can be of the greatest possible use in restoring also in the minds of the faithful the true concept of the Church.[1]

If only our people can be brought vividly to realise that to be a Christian means to have risen to new life with Christ in Baptism, to be united with the risen Christ and to share his divine life which courses through the entire Mystical Body, then they will once more realise truly what the Church is.

This does not mean that we have got to ignore the hierarchic structure of the Church. For, from the very beginning, Christ himself arranged that it should consist

1 Since Fr Jungmann wrote this passage a more complete restoration of the entire Holy Week liturgy has been decreed by Rome in 1955.—*Tr.*

of clergy and laity. In the prayer which immediately follows the Consecration, wherein there is said of the people the greatest possible thing that could be said of them—that they offer the holy sacrifice—the agent of the action is specified in the double expression: *nos servi tui sed et plebs tua sancta*. But clergy and people are lifted up together into an even higher unity; together with Christ they form the one People of God, the one Church.

Embellishment. Finally, if the sacrifice of the Church is to find adequate expression in action, we must always be on our guard against the tendency to embellishment, refinement or ornamentation. Of course we must not disdain all the various means of festivity and solemnisation to the glory of God on great occasions such as *Corpus Christi* and like feasts. But we should ever realise that for normal usage (that is, on ordinary Sundays) the finest ideal is not the maximum of splendour, but the worship of God 'in spirit and in truth', which means the utmost genuineness in the celebration. The prayer and sacrifice which goes up from all hearts, the praise which ascends to God from all mouths—sacrifice and praise terminating in sacramental completion by the Communion of as many as possible—that is the best solemnity.

In the ecclesiastical centres of every country it is right that we should have magnificent and impressive churches in which all the arts are employed to their best advantage. But for the normal parish of today what is needed is rather the small church, dignified but simple, in which a community can feel itself at home, in which the family feeling can grow, and in which the sacrifice of the Church can take shape and find expression.

The sacrifice of the Church must become discernible and recognisable in the concrete assembly of the faithful who *hic et nunc* are gathered about the altar.

As we pointed out in the beginning, to say of the Mass that it is the sacrifice of the Church is not to express its highest glory. It is a greater thing that the Mass is the sacrifice which the Church is able to offer *with Christ* to the glory of the heavenly Father.

IV

PHASES OF EUCHARISTIC WORSHIP

It is now some fifty years since St Pius X, in 1905, by a decree of the Sacred Congregation of the Council, took a step whereby a chapter in the history of Christian piety which had lasted for a thousand years was brought to an end, and the sacramental practice of early centuries was, in an important point, restored. From the date of this decree every Catholic who was in the state of grace and had a right intention was to be permitted, without other conditions, to receive Holy Communion frequently, even daily.

This decree was not the result of a sudden inspiration; it was the answer to a desire often though not unanimously expressed by enlightened theologians in the course of the nineteenth century. Nevertheless the decree occasioned great surprise, not only among the laity but also among the clergy. It was like a voice calling from another world; it spoke a language which was hardly understood. Only in the following decades, when the liturgical movement arose, did people get used to it; for this movement supplied the frame within which the picture became clear. A study of the train of thought expressed in the liturgy of the Mass as daily celebrated, and the logical consequence of these thoughts, leads naturally to the conclusion that if the Christian is to co-offer the sacrifice of Christ, he should obviously be able to share in the sacrificial meal; all the prayers of the Mass lead him to regard Communion as the daily bread of the children of God.

Those who thought deeply about the matter were of the opinion that the very circumstances of those days were such as to require this step of St Pius X. The Christian was no longer carried along by his *milieu* as he had been in former days; in many cases he had to assert himself against pagan surroundings. A situation like that of the early centuries of the Church, when Christians formed a minority, was taking shape once more, at least for the practising Catholic. For, although the number of nominal Christians may be legion in these days when almost everybody calls himself a Christian, there are in fact but few who really set themselves to seek first the Kingdom of God and his justice and to stake all for this cause. It had therefore become vital for Catholic life that there should be a concentration on essentials, a return to the very source from which that bygone heroic period had drawn its strength. The sun of the Eucharist must shine again with new brilliance.

There was, however, a certain difficulty which could soon be sensed, and which even today has not yet been overcome. It was that the Holy Eucharist already occupied a sovereign position in the life of piety of the Christian people and that a profusion of devotional practices in honour of the Blessed Sacrament existed, while at the same time these devotions were inspired by an attitude towards this sacred mystery quite different from that needed for welcome acceptance of the Pope's decree. Our fathers and forefathers believed as firmly as we do in the Real Presence of Christ in the Blessed Sacrament; they knew quite as well as we do what a precious legacy has been left to the Church; in fact their sense of reverence for the Blessed Sacrament seems to have exceeded that which is manifested by the average good Catholic of today.

But precisely in this point lies the difference. The sacramental piety of our fathers and forefathers of many past centuries was based on reverence and awe. They did not dare to make use of this sacrament after the fashion of the early Christians to whom 'taking part in the Mass' meant 'sharing in the sacrificial meal'. They regarded Communion as the special boon of a few great feasts, and held that Confession immediately before it was absolutely essential. Their prayer-books contained a whole anthology of 'Prayers before Communion' and 'Thanksgivings after Communion'; Communion thus seemed to them a thing apart from the Mass, a supreme devotion in itself; and they would not dare to allow children to approach the Lord's Table, no matter how pious and intelligent they might be, until they had reached the age of ten or twelve or (in some countries) fourteen years and had been prepared by a long and thorough course of instruction.

For this reason they laid all the greater stress on adoring and honouring the Holy Sacrament. To look up at the Host in adoration at the moment of the elevation was the basic form of eucharistic piety, except where it took the opposite form of not daring to look up, but of bowing down deeply instead—as was the custom in

France. This basic disposition assumed the most varied forms and was developed in different circumstances in all sorts of ways. People wanted the Sacred Host to be exposed to their gaze not merely at the elevation but during the entire Mass, since they were not accustomed to following the course of the Mass-ritual. Not only during Mass, but also during Vespers and all manner of devotions, the Blessed Sacrament had to be set up on its throne; special days and special hours were set apart for adoration; confraternities and sodalities came into being, devoted entirely to this purpose. In honour of the Blessed Sacrament a new feast was instituted, the feast of *Corpus Christi*. On this day the Sacred Host was to be carried in triumph through the streets of the town and through the fields all around the confines of the villages. It is clear that these and other devotional practices which have grown up in the Church since the thirteenth century are absolutely right, are firmly based on Catholic dogma and have been a great enrichment of the spiritual life of the people.

Especially since the Reformers of the sixteenth century attacked the doctrine of the Real Presence of our Lord in the Blessed Sacrament the reaction of the Church and her faithful children was obviously to defend the doctrine with all the greater zeal and devotion.

And yet it is impossible habitually to cultivate, with equal earnestness, two different forms of eucharistic piety. Now that we have returned on a wider basis to the normal use of the Sacrament we cannot at the same time maintain all the various substitutes as intensively as before. We cannot live in trustful intimacy with our eucharistic Lord and yet simultaneously keep at a reverential distance. We cannot attentively follow the whole course of the Mass, hearing the prayers and readings, providing the gifts, thanking, offering and receiving, while at the same time riveting our adoring gaze upon the monstrance.

On the other hand it is certain that we cannot push aside all that has grown up during a millenium. We cannot abolish the monstrance and do away with the tabernacle. We cannot give up *Corpus Christi* and Benediction of the Blessed Sacrament at the conclusion of our devotions. We must, however, be selective; and in many instances the selection has already been made for us by diocesan regulations.

In *diocesan* regulations: for laws relating to the Universal Church have ever shown a considerable restraint in this sphere of the cult of the Holy Eucharist. This is true especially as regards Exposition of the Blessed Sacrament during Mass. In the Code of Canon Law which enshrines older regulations Exposition is envisaged only at *Corpus Christi* and at the Forty Hours. These instances apart, Roman usage is never to have Exposition at the altar on which Mass is to be offered, but only on some other altar. This indicates the principle that the adoration of the Eucharist and the celebration of Mass should not be mixed up with each other;[1] for in Holy Mass, apart from the actual

1 At most the intermingling of two forms of devotion can be justified only on occasions like *Corpus Christi*, on the grounds that then the Blessed

moment of the Elevation, the Body of the Lord—though It is always handled with reverence—is not there to be adored, but to be offered and to be eaten. The adoration and thanks are offered to God as the beginning and the end of all things; it is to the Divine Majesty that the triple *Sanctus* is sung; that is of the essence of the sacrifice which is here offered to God. And Christ the God-man is standing with us to give power and value to our praying and offering. If, then, we desire to give fitting honour to the Sacrament of his Body, we should do it at another time and place, when this adoration can develop more freely.

Thus it shows a lack of understanding for the right order of things if pious souls regard the restriction of Masses before the Blessed Sacrament exposed as an impoverishment, even though they are ready to take advantage of the Church's more liberal dispensing of the eucharistic Bread, and perhaps even think that in their regrets they are influenced by the spirit of the liturgy.

On the other hand we have every reason to learn from the reverence wherewith former generations surrounded the Holy Eucharist. The fact that we can daily follow the Mass, missal in hand, and share in the Mass by our Communion without let or hindrance does not mean of itself that all is well. It is said that there are Catholics who do this as a matter of course day by day and year by year without, however, showing any fruits of it in their daily lives at home or work; Catholics who receive the

Sacrament is Itself the subject of the thanks which we are offering to God in the Mass.

Sacrament of Love as their daily Bread, yet remain as unloving as pagans; Catholics who are daily at the Holy Sacrifice, yet themselves show no spirit of sacrifice even to the extent of failing in the duties of their state of life.

The motto of St Pius X was 'To restore all things in Christ'. And by this he did not mean just the reception of the sacraments. The sacraments give us physical contact with Christ; but to this there must be added spiritual nearness to Christ, interior union with Christ and his principles, the formation in ourselves of 'that mind which was also in Christ Jesus', especially that mind wherewith he once offered and still continues to offer his sacrifice; and that is the spirit of a burning love for the heavenly Father, of selfless love for sinful humanity. With this spirit he draws us to himself in Holy Communion.

But if he wants thus to unite us with himself in sacrifice and Communion, his desire must be met by our own efforts. We ourselves must 'hunger and thirst after justice'. This hunger and thirst which should ever possess our souls has to be kept strong by our sedulous cultivation of prayer. And this does not mean merely saying prayers, even the best of prayers such as those which the Church offers to us in the missal. It means interior personal prayer, in meditation nourished by reading. And the chief subject of our reading should be the life of Christ as described to us in the Gospels; and to this should be added the rest of the New Testament which, especially in St Paul's Epistles, shows us the world in a new light, in the light of the glorified Christ.